My Brother Drew

by Sammie Witt

illustrated by Mike Dammer

Scott Foresman
is an imprint of

Glenview, Illinois • Boston, Massachusetts • Mesa, Arizona
Shoreview, Minnesota • Upper Saddle River, New Jersey

ISBN 13: 978-0-328-39333-6
ISBN 10:   0-328-39333-9

1 2 3 4 5 6 7 8 9 10 V010 17 16 15 14 13 12 11 10 09 08

Hi! I'm Sue. This is Drew. He is my little brother.

When Drew was born, he didn't do much. Now that he is big, he does a lot!

Drew can stand, but he needs help.
The other day, I saw him tugging on the
drapes to stand. I thought that would be
OK, but then, RIP!

"Mom," I yelled. "Come quick! I
need help!"

4

"I remember when you did that," she said to me. "I bet you can show Drew how to pull up on the sofa."

I took Drew to the sofa. He stood up.

Drew also likes to eat. He gets pretty messy.

I washed his face. He didn't like that at all. He threw his food.

"Mom," I yelled. "I need help!"

"I remember when you made a mess like that," she said to me. "Let Drew watch you wash your face."

I washed my face. Drew washed his face!

"See," said Mom. "You know what to do with Drew now."

Drew and I were looking at a picture book. The cat came in. Drew grabbed the cat. Drew likes the cat, but I'm not sure that the cat likes Drew.

"Dad," I yelled. "Come here! I need help!"

"I remember when you grabbed the cat like that," Dad said. "Can you show Drew the way to pet a cat?"

I took Drew's little hand and helped him pet the cat gently.

"See," Dad said. "You know what to do with Drew now."

Drew has had a busy day. He stood up. He made a mess. He grabbed the cat. Now he needs to sleep, but he isn't sleeping.

I have had a busy day too. I can't sleep. I can hear Drew crying in my room. I know what I can do, and I don't have to call for help this time.

I'll sing some quiet songs for Drew,
just like Mom and Dad did for me when
I was little. He likes that, just like I did.
See! I think he's going to sleep.
Good night.

As Babies Grow

Babies can be lots of fun. They can be lots of work, too, because they aren't able to do much for themselves. Parents, other family members, or babysitters must hold, feed, bathe, dress, and keep them safe and happy.

After babies grow a bit, and begin to walk, they are no longer babies but are toddlers. Toddlers learn to talk and to do many other things, but they still can't do many of the things you can do. As they grow, toddlers learn to do more and more by watching other people, like you, do things.

12